potatoes

COMFORT FOOD

potatoes

COMFORT FOOD

JANE STACEY

ANDREWS AND MCMEEL

A Universal Press Syndicate Company

KANSAS CITY

ISBN: 0-8362-2787-5

Library of Congress Catalog Card Number: 96-86725

First Edition

1 2 3 4 5 6 7 8 9 10

Produced by Smallwood & Stewart, Inc., New York City

Designer: Susi Oberhelman

Editor: Deborah Mintcheff

Photographer: Steven Mark Needham

Design Assistant: Ayako Hosono

Cover photograph: Garlic Smashed Potatoes, recipe on page 64.

Back cover photograph: Garlic Mashed Potato Shepherd's Pie, recipe on page 26.

Page 2 photograph: Roasted Potatoes with Lemon, recipe on page 76.

table of contents

Food fads come and go, but the potato remains a constant in all its incarnations. Unassuming and enduring, it has outlasted and outshone countless culinary trends and remains our favorite staple, whether we're eating at the corner luncheonette or dining at Lutèce. Roasted, fried, grilled, baked, sauteed, mashed, or boiled, in salads or in casseroles, as a snack or main dish—it's impossible not to love the earthy flavor and soothing, comforting qualities of the potato.

Potatoes are a complete food. They are rich in vitamins, minerals, and fiber, are low in fat, and contain appreciable amounts of protein. They are an

INTRODUCTION

excellent source of the type of complex carbohydrates our bodies need to help us sustain energy. To get the most nutrition from them, they should be scrubbed well and cooked with the skins on (most of the minerals are found just under the skin) but should not be overcooked or reheated.

Many varieties of potatoes are readily available today. They differ in appearance and flavor, but most importantly in the amount of starch they contain. At one end of the spectrum are the mealy-textured, high-starch varieties such as russets and Idahos, often labeled as baking potatoes. These oblong, rough, brown-skinned potatoes are best used for baking, mashing, or frying; because of their high starch content they lose their shape when boiled or steamed. At the opposite end of the spectrum are waxy-textured, low-starch potatoes that are usually smooth skinned, such as new potatoes, small red potatoes, fingerlings, round reds, and long whites. They are excellent boiled, grilled, steamed, and roasted because they contain more moisture and hold their shape well when cooked. All-purpose potatoes fall in the middle. They contain a medium amount of starch and are versatile enough to be mashed, boiled, roasted, or grilled. Yukon Gold, Yellow Finnish, and Peruvian Blues fall into this category.

Potatoes should always be stored in a well-ventilated, cool, dark place. At a temperature of about 50°F, they will keep for several weeks. Refrigerating potatoes is never recommended since at temperatures below 40°F they may develop a sweet flavor when their starch turns to sugar.

The dishes in this book form a true mosaic—my mother's mashed potatoes, a Spanish potato tortilla recipe handed down from a friend's grandmother, a favorite way of preparing Sunday-morning hash browns. Like the steadfastness of the potato itself, these are recipes I return to over and over again. I hope you will, too.

types of potatoes

Starch		Salads	Baking	Frying	Roasting/Grilling	Mashing	Boiling/Stews	Gratins
HIGH	• **Russet**		•	•		•		
	• **Idaho**		•	•		•		
	• **Baking**		•	•		•		
	• **Burbank**		•	•		•		
MEDIUM	• **Peruvian Blue**	•			•	•	•	•
	• **Yukon Gold**	•			•	•	•	•
	• **Yellow Finnish**	•			•	•	•	•
	• **Long White**	•			•		•	•
	• **White Rose**	•			•		•	•
	• **Eastern**	•			•		•	•
LOW	• **New Potatoes**	•			•		•	
	• **Le Rouge**	•			•		•	
	• **La Soda**	•			•		•	
	• **Fingerling**	•			•			
	• **Bintje**	•			•			
	• **Desiree**	•			•			

Weights

Ounces and Pounds	Metric Equivalents
¼ ounce	7 grams
⅓ ounce	10 g
½ ounce	14 g
1 ounce	28 g
1½ ounces	42 g
1¾ ounces	50 g
2 ounces	57 g
3 ounces	85 g
3½ ounces	100 g
4 ounces (¼ pound)	113 g
6 ounces	170 g
8 ounces (½ pound)	225 g
9 ounces	250 g
16 ounces (1 pound)	454 g

Temperatures

°F (Fahrenheit)	°C (Centigrade or Celsius)
32 (water freezes)	0
200	95
212 (water boils)	100
250	120
275	135
300 (slow oven)	150
325	160
350 (moderate oven)	175
375	190
400 (hot oven)	205
425	220
450 (very hot oven)	230
475	245
500 (extremely hot oven)	260

Liquid Measures

tsp.: teaspoon/Tbs.: tablespoon

Spoons and Cups	Metric Equivalents
¼ tsp.	1.23 milliliters
½ tsp.	2.5 ml
¾ tsp.	3.7 ml
1 tsp.	5 ml
1 dessertspoon	10 ml
1 Tbs. (3 tsp.)	15 ml
2 Tbs. (1 ounce)	30 ml
¼ cup	60 ml
⅓ cup	80 ml
½ cup	120 ml
⅔ cup	160 ml
¾ cup	180 ml
1 cup (8 ounces)	240 ml
2 cups (1 pint)	470 ml
3 cups	710 ml
4 cups (1 quart)	950 ml
4 quarts (1 gallon)	3.8 liters

Length

U.S. Measurements	Metric Equivalents
⅛ inch	3 mm
¼ inch	6 mm
⅜ inch	1 cm
½ inch	1.2 cm
¾ inch	2 cm
1 inch	2.5 cm
1¼ inches	3.1 cm
1½ inches	3.7 cm
2 inches	5 cm
3 inches	7.5 cm
4 inches	10 cm
5 inches	12.5 cm

Approximate Equivalents

1 kilogram is slightly more than 2 pounds
1 liter is slightly more than 1 quart
1 meter is slightly over 3 feet
1 centimeter is approximately ⅜ inch

thai sweet potato soup

Creamy coconut milk, tart lime juice,
and spicy red curry paste
blend beautifully with the mildness
of the sweet potatoes.

IN A LARGE POT, cover the sweet potatoes with water and bring to a boil. Cook over medium heat for about 20 minutes, or until tender. Drain.

In a small skillet, heat the oil over medium heat. Add the onions and cook, stirring occasionally, for 2 to 3 minutes, or until translucent. Remove from the heat and set aside.

In a food processor, puree the potatoes with the onions, in batches, until completely smooth. Transfer the potatoes to a large pot. Add the vegetable broth and coconut milk, stirring until smooth, and bring to a simmer over medium heat. Reduce the heat to low and stir in the lime juice, curry paste, coriander, and cloves. Season with salt and pepper. Simmer for 1 to 2 minutes. Ladle into soup bowls and garnish with cilantro. **SERVES 6 TO 8**

2 pounds sweet potatoes, peeled & cut into 1½-inch chunks

1 tablespoon vegetable oil

1 cup coarsely chopped onions

6 cups vegetable broth

1 (14-ounce) can unsweetened coconut milk

⅓ cup fresh lime juice

1 to 2 teaspoons Thai red curry paste

½ teaspoon ground coriander

⅛ teaspoon ground cloves

Salt & freshly ground pepper

Fresh cilantro leaves, for garnish

potato-seafood chowder

2 tablespoons butter

1 cup coarsely chopped
leeks (white part only)

1 cup thinly sliced celery

2 garlic cloves, finely
chopped

1¾ pounds russet
potatoes, peeled &
cut into ½-inch dice

4 cups chicken broth

1 cup dry white wine

2 (8-ounce) bottles
clam juice

1 bay leaf

Seafood chowder recipes often call for a homemade fish stock which, while delicious, is time-consuming. Here the base is a lighter-flavored blend of white wine, chicken broth, and clam juice that allows the delicate flavors of the seafood to shine through.

IN A LARGE POT, melt the butter over medium heat. Add the leeks, celery, and garlic and saute for 3 to 4 minutes, or until softened, but not yet browned. Add the potatoes, stirring well to coat them with the butter. Stir in the broth and wine and bring to a boil. Reduce the heat to low and let simmer for 15 minutes, or until the potatoes are fork-tender.

Stir in the clam juice and bay leaf. Increase the heat to medium. When the soup returns to a simmer, add the shrimp, salmon, and scallops. Cook for 3 to 4 minutes, or until the seafood is just cooked through and no longer translucent in the center. Reduce the heat to low.

Add the heavy cream, peas, parsley, and thyme, gently stirring to combine. Season with salt and pepper. When the chowder is hot, ladle into heated soup bowls. Garnish with the diced tomato. **SERVES 6 TO 8**

potato-corn chowder

Omit the clam juice, shrimp, salmon, scallops, and peas. After adding the bay leaf and returning the soup to a simmer, add 2 cups fresh or frozen corn kernels. Add 2 teaspoons chopped fresh dill with the heavy cream, parsley, and thyme.

SERVES 4

¾ pound medium-size shrimp, peeled & deveined

½ pound salmon fillet, skinned & cut into ¾-inch pieces

½ pound bay scallops

1½ cups heavy cream

1½ cups frozen baby peas, thawed

⅓ cup finely chopped fresh parsley

2 teaspoons finely chopped fresh thyme

Salt & freshly ground pepper

1 cup seeded & diced tomato, for garnish

country-style potato-leek soup

This classic French country winter soup is simplicity itself—just leeks and potatoes in a tasty broth.

- **½ cup (1 stick) butter**

- **4 cups thinly sliced leeks (white part only)**

- **1¾ pounds potatoes (any type), peeled & cut into 1-inch chunks**

- **6 cups chicken or vegetable broth**

- **1 cup dry white wine**

- **Salt & freshly ground pepper**

- **Coarsely chopped fresh parsley, for garnish (optional)**

IN A LARGE POT, melt the butter over medium heat. Add the leeks and cook for 5 to 8 minutes, or until wilted. Add the potatoes, broth, and wine. Bring to a boil, then reduce the heat to low and simmer, covered, for 20 to 25 minutes, or until the potatoes are tender when pierced with a fork. Season with salt and pepper. Ladle into heated soup bowls, and garnish with chopped parsley, if using. **SERVES 6 TO 8**

southwestern baked potatoes

*Salty, sharp Cheddar cheese and
the heat of jalapeños mix
it up with the mild taste of russets
in this one-dish supper.*

PREHEAT THE OVEN to 400°F. Use a fork to prick the potatoes in several places. Place on the center rack of the oven. Bake for 1 hour and 15 minutes, or until easily pierced with a fork.

Prepare the salsa fresca: In a small bowl, combine the tomatoes, scallions, jalapeño, cilantro, garlic, lime juice, and oil. Season with salt and pepper and mix well. Set aside.

To serve, use a paring knife to cut a lengthwise slit in each potato; use a fork to open up the potatoes. Sprinkle some cheese into each potato, top with a heaping tablespoon of salsa, and garnish with cilantro. Serve the remaining salsa alongside.

SERVES 4

4 large russet potatoes (about 12 ounces each), scrubbed

SALSA FRESCA

1½ cups seeded & diced tomatoes

¼ cup chopped scallions

1 or 2 jalapeño chiles, seeded & finely chopped

3 tablespoons finely chopped fresh cilantro

1 garlic clove, finely chopped

2 tablespoons fresh lime juice

2 tablespoons olive oil

Salt & freshly ground pepper

1 cup grated Cheddar cheese (4 ounces)

Fresh cilantro leaves, for garnish

TIP

When you're in a hurry, microwaving potatoes sometimes makes more sense than baking. Scrub 2 large baking potatoes and prick in several places with a fork. Place on a double layer of paper towels and microwave on High for 6 minutes. Turn the potatoes upside down and microwave 6 to 10 minutes more, until they are tender when pierced with a fork. Cover and let sit 10 minutes before serving.

gorgonzola baked potatoes

Bake 4 large russet potatoes as directed. Meanwhile, in a small bowl, combine 8 ounces smoked chicken, cut into 1-inch slivers, 6 ounces Gorgonzola cheese, crumbled, and 1 tablespoon chopped sun-dried tomatoes. When the potatoes are tender, slit them and open. Top each potato with the smoked chicken and Gorgonzola mixture.   **SERVES 4**

baked potatoes with brie

Bake 4 large russet potatoes as directed. When the potatoes are tender, slit them and open. Divide 4 ounces Black Forest ham, cut into ¼-inch-wide strips, among the potatoes. Top with 8 ounces Brie cheese, cut into ¼-inch cubes. Use a fork to lightly mash the Brie. Place on a baking sheet. Bake in the 400°F oven for 8 minutes, or until the Brie begins to melt.   **SERVES 4**

twice-baked potatoes

Sour cream is a natural with baked potatoes. Here it's enlivened with fresh dill and chives and spiked with just a hint of Dijon mustard.

PREHEAT THE OVEN to 400°F. Use a fork to prick the potatoes in several places. Bake for about 1 hour and 15 minutes, or until tender. Remove from the oven and increase the oven temperature to 425°F.

In a medium-size bowl, combine the sour cream, Parmesan, mustard, dill, and chives. Season with salt and pepper. Set aside.

Make a lengthwise slit in each potato and scoop the flesh into the bowl with the sour cream mixture, reserving the potato shells. Mash the potato flesh with the sour cream mixture until thoroughly blended. Spoon the potato mixture back into the potato shells, dividing it evenly. Top each potato with a sprinkling of paprika and place the potatoes on a baking sheet.

Bake the potatoes for 12 to 14 minutes, or until the tops are beginning to brown. Serve immediately. **SERVES 4**

4 large russet potatoes (about 12 ounces each), scrubbed

½ cup sour cream

3 tablespoons freshly grated Parmesan cheese

1 tablespoon Dijon mustard

2 teaspoons snipped fresh dill

2 teaspoons snipped fresh chives

Salt & freshly ground pepper

Sweet Hungarian paprika, for sprinkling

twice-baked sweet potatoes

- 4 sweet potatoes
  (about 10 ounces each),
  scrubbed

- ⅓ cup plus 1 tablespoon
  freshly grated
  Parmesan cheese

- ¼ cup (½ stick) butter,
  cut into small pieces

- 2 teaspoons finely
  chopped fresh sage

- 2 teaspoons crushed red
  pepper flakes

- 2 teaspoons pure
  chile powder
  (mild or medium-hot)

- Salt & freshly ground
  pepper

- Coarsely chopped
  roasted cashews,
  for garnish

I love this sweet potato version of twice-baked potatoes. It combines butter and Parmesan cheese with fresh sage and red chile, and is garnished with roasted cashews.

PREHEAT THE OVEN to 400°F. With a small knife, prick the potatoes in several places. Bake for 1 hour and 15 minutes, or until tender. Remove from the oven and increase the oven temperature to 425°F.

Make a lengthwise slit in each potato and scoop the potato flesh into a bowl, reserving the potato shells. Mash the potatoes with the Parmesan, butter, sage, red pepper flakes, and chile powder. Season with salt and pepper. Spoon the potato mixture back into the potato shells, dividing it evenly. Place on a baking sheet.

Bake for 12 minutes, or until the tops are beginning to brown. Sprinkle with the cashews and serve immediately.

SERVES 4

spanish tortilla with saffron-tomato sauce

Almost every tapas bar in Spain serves some kind of tortilla a la Española, a simple potato omelet much like a frittata. This one is cut into thick wedges and served with a light tomato sauce with green olives. It makes a great light lunch or brunch.

PREPARE THE SAFFRON-tomato sauce: In a small skillet, heat the oil over medium heat. Add the onion and saute for 2 to 3 minutes, or until soft. Add the garlic and cook for 10 to 15 seconds. Add the wine and saffron. Reduce the heat to low and stir in the tomatoes, olives, and parsley. Season with salt and pepper. Transfer the sauce to a small serving bowl and keep warm.

In a medium-size saucepan, cover the potatoes with water and bring to a boil. Reduce the heat to medium and cook for 12 to 15 minutes, or until just tender. Drain and pat dry. Set aside.

In a large bowl, beat the eggs until foamy. Stir in the potatoes, Parmesan, and parsley. Season with salt and pepper.

SAFFRON-TOMATO SAUCE

2 tablespoons olive oil

¼ cup chopped onion

1 garlic clove, thinly sliced

¼ cup dry white wine

A few saffron threads

3 plum tomatoes, diced

2 tablespoons sliced pimiento-stuffed green olives

1 tablespoon finely chopped fresh parsley

Salt & freshly ground pepper

1½ pounds potatoes (any type), peeled & cut into ⅛-inch-thick slices

4 large eggs

In a large heavy skillet with sloping sides, heat the oil over medium heat, tilting the pan to thoroughly coat the sides with oil. Add the onion and cook for 2 to 3 minutes, or until softened. Increase the heat to high and heat the pan for 10 seconds. Add the egg mixture, tilting the pan to distribute the eggs evenly. Using a spatula, spread the potatoes evenly in the pan. Reduce the heat to medium and cook for 3 to 4 minutes, or until the underside of the tortilla begins to brown.

Use a narrow metal spatula to loosen the tortilla from the sides of the pan. Invert a large plate over the tortilla and turn the skillet over to release the tortilla. Gently slide the tortilla back into the skillet. Cook for 3 to 4 minutes, or until brown on the second side. Transfer to a serving plate. Cut the tortilla into wedges and serve hot, accompanied by the tomato sauce.

SERVES 4

¼ cup freshly grated Parmesan cheese

2 tablespoons finely chopped fresh parsley

Salt & freshly ground pepper

3 tablespoons olive oil

½ cup chopped onion

artichoke & parmesan frittata

This hearty frittata has lots of sliced potatoes, sweet artichoke hearts, and just enough eggs to hold it together.

1½ pounds small potatoes (any type)

2 tablespoons olive oil

1 cup coarsely chopped onions

1 roasted red bell pepper, peeled, cored, seeded & cut into ¼-inch-wide strips

1 (15-ounce) can artichoke hearts, drained & quartered

2 tablespoons chopped fresh basil

2 tablespoons chopped fresh parsley

12 large eggs

⅓ cup freshly grated Parmesan cheese

½ teaspoon salt

¼ teaspoon freshly ground pepper

IN A LARGE SAUCEPAN, cover the potatoes with water. Bring to a boil and cook for about 15 minutes, or until tender. Drain and let cool slightly. Peel and cut into ¼-inch-thick slices. Set aside.

Preheat the oven to 350°F. Generously grease a 13-by-9-inch baking dish. Set aside.

In a large heavy skillet, heat the oil over medium heat. Add the onions and saute for 3 to 4 minutes, or until softened. Spread in the prepared dish. Add the potatoes to the skillet; cook for 3 to 5 minutes, turning them, until browned.

Arrange the potatoes over the onions. Scatter the roasted pepper, artichoke hearts, basil, and parsley on top.

In a medium-size bowl, whisk the remaining ingredients. Pour over the vegetables. Bake for 30 to 35 minutes, just until the eggs are set. Serve hot or warm. **SERVES 8**

ham & scalloped potatoes

*I always add ham to scalloped
potatoes. Its smoky flavor
transforms this simple main dish into
something special—and it
tastes even better the next day.*

PREHEAT THE OVEN
to 350°F. Halve the potatoes lengthwise, then cut them
crosswise into ¼-inch-thick slices. Place in a 2-quart casserole
and add the ham.

In a medium-size saucepan, melt the butter over medium
heat. Add the flour, whisking constantly, until the mixture is
thickened and bubbling. Slowly add the milk, whisking
constantly, and cook, whisking often, until the sauce thickens and comes to a boil. Reduce the heat to low and add the
mustard, salt, and pepper. Cook for 2 to 3 minutes.

Pour the sauce over the potatoes and ham and stir to coat.
Bake, covered, for 1½ hours or until the potatoes are tender. Let
stand, uncovered, for 15 minutes before serving. **SERVES 8**

**1¾ pounds russet or
Yukon Gold potatoes,
peeled**

**¾ pound good-quality
smoked ham, cut into
bite-size chunks**

3 tablespoons butter

**3 tablespoons
all-purpose flour**

2½ cups milk

**1 tablespoon Dijon
mustard**

¼ teaspoon salt

**⅛ teaspoon freshly
ground pepper**

mediterranean pizza

2 (6-ounce) Yukon Gold potatoes, peeled & cut into ¼-inch-thick slices

2 tablespoons chopped sun-dried tomatoes

4 garlic cloves

2 tablespoons coarsely chopped fresh basil

1 tablespoon fresh rosemary

1 tablespoon fresh oregano

¼ teaspoon salt

¼ teaspoon freshly ground pepper

¼ cup extra-virgin olive oil

1 (12-inch) prebaked thin pizza crust

4 ounces feta cheese

8 cherry tomatoes, halved

8 oil-cured olives, pitted

½ cup freshly grated Parmesan cheese

Sealed beneath the potato topping is a fragrant blend of tomatoes, basil, rosemary, oregano, and garlic.

IN A SMALL POT, cover the potato slices with water and bring to a boil. Cook over medium heat for 12 to 15 minutes, or until just tender. Drain, rinse briefly under cold water, and drain thoroughly.

Preheat the oven to 450°F.

In a food processor, pulse the sun-dried tomatoes, garlic, basil, rosemary, oregano, salt, and pepper until a chunky paste forms. Slowly add the oil and process until the mixture forms a coarse puree.

Place the crust on a baking sheet and spread with the herb paste, leaving a ½-inch border. Arrange the potatoes on top in overlapping concentric circles. Top with the crumbled feta cheese, cherry tomatoes, and olives. Sprinkle with the Parmesan.

Bake for 12 to 14 minutes, or until the cheese is melted and the potatoes are lightly browned. **SERVES 4**

garlic mashed potato shepherd's pie

I've always loved the taste of cumin seed and the heat of red peppers in lamb stews, so I thought I'd try them in shepherd's pie. Goat cheese in the potato topping adds creaminess and a real tang.

¾ cup all-purpose flour

Salt & freshly ground pepper

2¼ pounds boneless leg of lamb, trimmed & cut into ¾-inch pieces

3 to 5 tablespoons olive oil or more, if needed

4 garlic cloves, chopped

1½ cups dry white wine

1 cup water

2½ cups thinly sliced carrots

1 pint pearl onions, peeled

PREHEAT THE OVEN to 350°F. In a pie plate, combine the flour, ¼ teaspoon salt, and ⅛ teaspoon pepper. Dredge the lamb pieces in the flour until well coated.

In a large heavy skillet, heat 3 tablespoons oil. Brown the lamb, in batches, over medium-high heat for 2 to 3 minutes, using additional oil as needed. Transfer the lamb to a medium-size bowl and set aside.

Reduce the heat to medium, add the garlic, and cook for about 1 minute. Pour in the wine and water, stirring to scrape up any brown bits from the bottom of the skillet. Add the

Photograph on back cover

carrots and onions and bring to a boil. Reduce the heat to low and simmer, partially covered, for 10 minutes.

Stir in the bay leaves, thyme, cumin, and red pepper flakes, if using. Season with salt and pepper. Add the lamb and cook for 3 to 4 minutes, stirring, until the cooking liquid has thickened. Transfer to a 2-quart casserole or baking dish.

Use a potato masher to mash the potatoes until smooth. Spoon the potatoes over the top of the lamb. Bake, uncovered, for 30 to 35 minutes. Top with the crumbled goat cheese and bake for 10 to 15 minutes more, or until the cheese has softened and the potatoes are golden. Remove from the oven and let rest 10 minutes before serving. **SERVES 6 TO 8**

2 bay leaves

2 teaspoons chopped fresh thyme

½ teaspoon cumin seeds

½ teaspoon crushed red pepper flakes (optional)

½ recipe Garlic Smashed Potatoes (p. 64; omit the shallots)

½ cup crumbled mild goat cheese, such as Montrachet (about 3 ounces)

pesto potatoes with pasta

Frozen pesto is fine for stirring into minestrone soup or enriching a tomato sauce, but in this dish use the freshest, most fragrant basil you can find.

PESTO

1¼ cups fresh basil leaves

3 tablespoons freshly grated Parmesan cheese, plus extra for serving

2 garlic cloves

⅓ cup olive oil

PREPARE THE PESTO: In a food processor, combine the basil, Parmesan, and garlic and process until finely chopped. With the machine running, gradually add the oil, and process until a coarse puree has formed. Set aside.

If using Russian banana potatoes, halve them lengthwise. If using Bintjes or red potatoes, cut them into ⅛-inch-thick slices.

In a medium-size saucepan, cover the potatoes with water and bring to a boil. Cook over medium heat for 8 to 10 minutes, or until just tender when pierced with a fork. Drain the potatoes. Set aside.

Bring a large pot of water to a rolling boil. Drop the pasta into the boiling water and stir once or twice. After the water returns to a boil, cook for 10 to 12 minutes, or until the pasta is al dente. Drain immediately in a colander, then drizzle with the oil, shaking the colander to thoroughly coat the pasta.

In a large skillet, melt the butter over medium heat. Add the wine and the pesto. Stir in the potatoes and pasta, season with salt and pepper. Toss gently to combine, and transfer to a serving dish. Sprinkle with basil and serve. Pass the grated Parmesan separately. **SERVES 4 TO 6**

cold pesto-potato pasta salad

Omit the butter, wine, and Parmesan. Cook the potatoes as directed; drain and place in a large bowl. Cook the pasta as directed, but rinse under cold water and drain well before drizzling with the oil; put into the bowl with the potatoes. Add the pesto and 1 recipe Simple Mayonnaise, (p. 48) toss well to coat, and season with salt and pepper. Transfer to a serving bowl and garnish with julienned basil.

1 pound potatoes, such as Russian banana, Bintjes, or other small potatoes, scrubbed

12 ounces bow-tie pasta

3 tablespoons olive oil

3 tablespoons unsalted butter

3 tablespoons dry white wine

Salt & freshly ground pepper

Julienned fresh basil, for garnish

gruyère & goat cheese tart

1 cup all-purpose flour

¼ teaspoon salt

6 tablespoons cold unsalted butter, cut into 8 pieces

¼ cup grated Gruyère cheese

3 to 4 tablespoons lightly beaten egg

Peruvian Blue potatoes, despite their unusual bluish purple flesh, have a flavor similar to most other potatoes.

PREPARE THE PASTRY: In a food processor, combine the flour, salt, and butter. Pulse until the mixture is crumbly. Add the Gruyère and pulse twice to incorporate. Still pulsing, add enough beaten egg to form the dough into a ball. On a lightly floured surface, knead the dough once or twice. Shape into a disk, wrap in plastic wrap, and refrigerate for at least 20 minutes, or up to 1 day.

Prepare the potato filling: In a medium-size saucepan, cover the potatoes with water and bring to a boil. Cook over medium heat for about 15 minutes, or until tender when pierced with a fork. Drain and cool. Cut the unpeeled potatoes into ¼-inch-thick slices. Set aside.

In a skillet, melt 2 tablespoons of the butter over medium

heat. Saute the leeks for 2 to 3 minutes, or until softened. Add the wine; remove from the heat. Stir in the rosemary; set aside.

Preheat the oven to 375°F.

On a lightly floured surface, roll the dough into a 13-inch round. Fit the dough into a 10-inch tart pan with a removable bottom, folding the edges over twice to reinforce the sides. Press the dough so it extends slightly above the rim of the pan. Spread the leeks over the dough. Sprinkle with the Gruyère and crumble the goat cheese on top. Season with salt and pepper. Arrange the potatoes in concentric circles on top, slightly overlapping the slices. Melt the remaining 2 tablespoons butter and brush over the potatoes.

Bake for 30 to 35 minutes, or until the tart shell is golden and the goat cheese is bubbly. Cool for 10 minutes, then remove the pan sides. Serve hot, warm, or cold. **SERVES 6 TO 8**

POTATO FILLING

1 pound Peruvian Blue potatoes, scrubbed

¼ cup (½ stick) butter

2 cups thinly sliced leeks (white part only)

3 tablespoons dry white wine

2 teaspoons chopped fresh rosemary

1 cup grated Gruyère cheese (4 ounces)

4 ounces mild goat cheese

Salt & freshly ground pepper

llapingachos

*In Ecuador, these spicy cheese
and potato patties are daily fare at
every meal, and are usually
served with fried eggs. My recipe is
lighter on the cheese and calls
for cilantro and corn for extra flavor.*

IN A LARGE SAUCEPAN, cover the potatoes with water and bring to a boil. Cook over medium heat for 15 minutes, or until tender. Drain and return to the pan. Stir gently over medium heat for about 1 minute.

Put the potatoes into a large bowl and mash until smooth. Stir in the corn, cheese, chile, scallions, and the cilantro, if using. Season with salt and pepper and mix well. Shape into 8 patties about ¾ inch thick.

In a large heavy skillet, melt the butter. In 2 batches, cook the patties over medium heat, turning once, for 6 to 8 minutes, or until golden brown. Remove to a heated serving platter. Pass the garnishes separately. **SERVES 4 TO 6**

1¾ pounds russet or Yukon Gold potatoes, peeled & cut into 1-inch chunks

⅔ cup fresh corn kernels, or thawed if frozen

½ cup grated Monterey Jack cheese

1 Anaheim or poblano chile, seeded & chopped

⅓ cup chopped scallions

3 tablespoons chopped fresh cilantro (optional)

Salt & freshly ground pepper

3 tablespoons butter

all-american potato salad

3 pounds russet or
Yukon Gold potatoes

3 hard-boiled eggs,
coarsely chopped

1 cup diced celery

¾ cup diced green
bell pepper

½ cup diced red onion

½ cup finely chopped
fresh parsley

1¾ cups mayonnaise

2 tablespoons Dijon
mustard

2 tablespoons cider
vinegar

2 teaspoons sugar
(optional)

Salt & freshly ground
pepper

Paprika, for sprinkling
(optional)

*The secret to this salad's
comforting, creamy texture
is tossing the potatoes with
the mayonnaise dressing while
the potatoes are still warm.*

IN A LARGE POT, cover the potatoes with water. Bring to a boil and cook over medium heat for 35 to 40 minutes, or until tender when pierced with a small knife. Drain the potatoes and let them cool slightly, then peel.

Quarter the potatoes lengthwise, then cut into ¼-inch-thick slices. Place the potatoes in a large bowl along with the eggs, celery, bell pepper, onion, and parsley. Set aside.

In a small bowl, whisk together the mayonnaise, mustard, vinegar, and the sugar, if using. Spoon the dressing over the potatoes. Gently mix to combine. Season with salt and pepper, then sprinkle with paprika, if desired. **SERVES 6 TO 8**

german potato salad

*This potato salad, served warm or hot
from the oven, was always served at
family outings when I was growing up.*

IN A LARGE POT,
cover the potatoes with water. Bring to a boil and cook over
medium heat for 20 to 25 minutes, or until tender; drain. Peel and
cut lengthwise in half, then crosswise into ¼-inch-thick slices. Put
the potatoes into a 3-quart baking dish. Set aside.

Preheat the oven to 350°F. In a large heavy skillet, cook the
bacon over medium heat until crisp. Drain the bacon, let cool,
then crumble. Discard all but 3 tablespoons of the drippings. Add
the onions to the skillet and cook over medium heat, stirring, for 4
minutes, or until softened. Whisk in the flour. Gradually add the
water, whisking until smooth. Stir in the vinegar and sugar. When
bubbling and thick, remove from the heat and pour over the potatoes. Add the bacon and parsley, season with salt and pepper, and
gently mix. Cover the casserole and bake for 30 minutes. Uncover
and bake for 15 minutes longer, or until the edges are golden.

SERVES 6 TO 8

3 pounds russet or
  Yukon Gold potatoes

6 slices thick-cut bacon

1½ cups chopped onions

¼ cup all-purpose flour

2½ cups water

¾ cup cider vinegar

3 tablespoons sugar

⅓ cup chopped
  fresh parsley

Salt & freshly
  ground pepper

grilled potato salad with lemon & mint

Fresh lemon juice, oregano, and mint gives this salad a decidedly Greek twist.

1¾ pounds small new potatoes, halved

1 each red and yellow bell pepper, halved, cored & seeded

1 medium-size zucchini, halved lengthwise

1 small red onion, quartered

¼ cup olive oil

Juice of 1 lemon

2 tablespoons coarsely chopped fresh parsley

1 tablespoon finely chopped fresh oregano

2 teaspoons finely chopped fresh mint

½ teaspoon crushed red pepper flakes

Salt & freshly ground pepper

PREHEAT A GAS GRILL to medium or prepare a medium-hot charcoal fire.

In a large saucepan, cover the potatoes with water and bring to a boil. Cook over medium heat for 15 minutes, or until almost cooked through. Drain.

Put the potatoes, bell peppers, zucchini, and onion into a large bowl. Toss with 2 tablespoons of the oil.

Grill the vegetables, turning occasionally, for 3 to 4 minutes, or until tender and nicely marked.

Cut the bell peppers into ½-inch-wide strips. Cut the zucchini into ½-inch-thick slices. Coarsely chop the onion. Add to the bowl along with the remaining 2 tablespoons oil, lemon juice, parsley, oregano, mint, and red pepper flakes. Season with salt and pepper and toss until mixed. Serve warm.

SERVES 4 TO 6

summer corn & potato salad

Splashing hot potatoes with white wine adds a zesty flavor and keeps them moist. Pan-roasting gives corn a slightly nutty flavor and keeps it sweet and crisp.

IN A LARGE POT, cover the potatoes with water and bring to a boil. Cook over medium heat for 15 minutes, or until tender. Drain. Put the hot potatoes into a large bowl; sprinkle with the wine. Set aside.

In a large skillet, place the corn over medium-high heat. Cook for 3 to 4 minutes, stirring, until the corn begins to make popping sounds. Transfer to the bowl with the potatoes. Add the chopped basil, parsley, scallions, and capers.

In a small bowl, whisk together the vinegar, mustard, and lemon juice. Slowly whisk in the oil until thickened. Pour the vinaigrette over the potato mixture, season with salt and pepper, and toss to coat. Gently stir in the tomatoes. Serve the day it is made. **SERVES 6 TO 8**

3 pounds small new potatoes, scrubbed & halved

⅓ cup dry white wine

1½ cups fresh corn kernels

¼ cup each chopped fresh basil, parsley & scallions

1 tablespoon capers

3 tablespoons white wine vinegar

1 tablespoon Dijon mustard

1 tablespoon lemon juice

⅔ cup olive oil

Salt & pepper

3 plum tomatoes, quartered

5 to 8 cherry tomatoes, halved

perfect french fries

A Parisian chef taught me how to make proper French fries: The potatoes are first fried at a low temperature to cook them through. Then they are fried at a much higher temperature to produce their glorious golden-brown color and to crisp them.

2½ pounds large baking potatoes, peeled

Vegetable oil for deep-frying

Salt (optional)

Homemade Ketchup (p. 49), mustard, or malt vinegar

NOTE

Malt vinegar is a mild-flavored vinegar made from malted barley. It is the condiment of choice in England for fries (called chips).

CUT THE POTATOES lengthwise into ½-inch-thick slices. Stack the slices, a few at a time, and cut them lengthwise into ¼-inch-wide sticks. As you cut the potatoes, put them into a bowl of lukewarm water for about 10 minutes. Drain, then rinse well. Pat the potatoes dry. Wrap them in a clean kitchen towel and set aside.

In a deep-fryer, wok, or large heavy pot with high sides, heat 3 to 4 inches of oil (the oil should not reach more than halfway up the pot sides) to 325°F *(see Note, p. 42)*. Add a small batch of potatoes (about 12), and fry for 4 to 6 minutes, just until they begin to color. Use a wire strainer or tongs to remove

NOTE

If you don't have a deep-fry/candy thermometer, you can judge the temperature of the oil by watching its surface. When it begins to shimmer, it is about 325°F.

At 350°F to 380°F a small cube of white bread will rise to the surface 3 to 5 seconds after being dropped into the oil, turning an even golden color.

the fries and drain on paper towels. Continue to fry the potatoes in small batches. Let the fries cool to room temperature. (They can be set aside for up to 2 hours.)

Add more oil if necessary and reheat to 380°F (*see Note*). Working in small batches, and allowing the oil to reach 380°F before adding each new batch, fry the potatoes for 2 to 3 minutes, or until brown and crisp. Drain the fries briefly on paper towels. Sprinkle with salt, if desired. Serve immediately, accompanied by ketchup, mustard, or a sprinkling of malt vinegar. **SERVES 4 TO 6**

herb-coated steak fries

These delicious fries are wrapped in a crust of dried herbs, cumin, paprika, and salt.

PREHEAT THE OVEN to 475°F. Cut the potatoes lengthwise in half, then cut crosswise in half. Place the potatoes, cut side down, on a work surface. Cut lengthwise into ½-inch-thick slices. Place the potatoes on a large baking sheet. Drizzle with the oil, tossing to coat evenly.

In a small bowl, combine the remaining ingredients. Sprinkle the spice mixture over the potatoes, and toss to coat evenly. Arrange the potatoes in a single layer on the baking sheet.

Bake the potatoes for 20 minutes. Use a spatula to loosen and turn the potatoes. Bake for 20 to 25 minutes more, or until the edges are browned. Serve immediately. **SERVES 6**

2 large russet potatoes (about 1½ pounds), scrubbed

2 large sweet potatoes (about 1¼ pounds), scrubbed

3 tablespoons vegetable oil

1 teaspoon ground cumin

½ teaspoon dried oregano

½ teaspoon paprika

½ teaspoon salt

½ teaspoon dried thyme

¼ teaspoon dried rosemary

¼ teaspoon freshly ground pepper

¼ teaspoon ground red pepper (optional)

low-fat oven fries

2¾ pounds russet potatoes, peeled

2 tablespoons vegetable oil

¼ to ½ teaspoon salt

With only two tablespoons of oil for four to six servings, these fries nearly qualify as health food!

PREHEAT THE OVEN to 475°F. Cut the potatoes lengthwise into ½-inch-thick slices. Stack the slices, a few at a time, and cut them lengthwise into ½-inch-wide sticks. Place the potato sticks on a baking sheet. Toss with the oil and salt and spread in a single layer.

Bake the potatoes for 15 minutes, or until browned on the bottom. Turn the potatoes over with a spatula. Continue baking for about 10 minutes longer, or until cooked through and golden brown. Serve immediately. **SERVES 6**

matchstick potatoes

For an elegant dish, pile these high in the center of a serving plate with thinly sliced beef tenderloin and steamed summer squash on either side.

1½ pounds russet potatoes, peeled

Vegetable oil for deep-frying

Salt (optional)

USING A SHARP KNIFE or a vegetable slicer, cut the potatoes into ⅛-inch-thick slices. Stack the slices, a few at a time, and cut lengthwise into ⅛-inch-wide sticks. Put the potatoes into a bowl of lukewarm water and soak for 2 to 3 minutes. Drain the potatoes, then rinse well. Pat dry with paper towels and gently wrap in a clean kitchen towel.

In a deep-fryer, wok, or large heavy pot with high sides, heat 2 to 3 inches of oil (the oil should not reach more than halfway up the sides of the pot) to 375°F (*see Note, p. 42*). Fry the potatoes, in small batches, for 30 seconds to 1 minute, or until crisp and golden. Drain on paper towels. Sprinkle with salt, if desired. Serve immediately. **SERVES 4 TO 6**

heavenly potato chips

I fry white and sweet potato chips separately because the sweet tend to take a second or two longer to cook. Once cooked, their edges turn dark brown very quickly.

1 baking potato (about 8 ounces), peeled

1 sweet potato (about 8 ounces), peeled

Vegetable oil, for deep-frying

Salt

USING A LARGE SHARP KNIFE or a vegetable slicer, cut the potatoes into $\frac{1}{16}$-inch-thick slices. In separate bowls, soak the white and sweet potato slices in lukewarm water for 2 minutes. Rinse and dry thoroughly.

In a large heavy pot with high sides, heat 3 to 4 inches of oil (the oil should not reach more than halfway up the sides of the pot) to 375°F *(see Note, p. 42)*. Fry the potatoes, in very small batches, for 45 seconds to 1 minute, or until crisp and golden. Using a wire strainer, remove the chips and drain on paper towels. Sprinkle with salt. Be sure to allow the oil to reach 375°F, before adding each new batch. These are best when eaten within two hours after being made. **SERVES 4**

simple mayonnaise

1 large egg

1 large egg yolk

3 tablespoons fresh lemon juice

¼ teaspoon salt

⅛ teaspoon ground pepper

¾ cup plus 2 tablespoons vegetable oil

2 tablespoons olive oil

I like to think of mayonnaise as a basic sauce with endless possibilities. Try dipping homemade French fries into the Hot-&-Spicy Mayonnaise.

IN A FOOD PROCESSOR, combine the egg, egg yolk, lemon juice, salt, and pepper. Process for 20 to 30 seconds, or until blended. With the machine running, pour in the oils in a very slow, steady stream, and process until thoroughly incorporated and the mixture is thick. Store in the refrigerator for up to 3 days. **MAKES 1 CUP**

hot-&-spicy mayonnaise

Substitute 3 tablespoons fresh lime juice for the lemon juice. Add 1 garlic clove, chopped, 1 teaspoon crushed red pepper flakes, and 1½ teaspoons mild or medium-hot chile powder to the egg mixture. After the mayonnaise is prepared, stir in 2 tablespoons chopped fresh cilantro.

homemade ketchup

The deep, sweet flavor of balsamic vinegar and the nutty taste of dark sesame oil transform store-bought ketchup into a special condiment that's perfect with French fries.

¼ cup balsamic vinegar

½ cup ketchup

2 teaspoons dark sesame oil

2 to 3 drops Tabasco sauce

IN A SMALL SAUCEPAN, bring the vinegar to a boil over medium heat. Reduce the heat to low and simmer until reduced to 2 tablespoons. (It will resemble molasses.) Remove from the heat and use a rubber spatula to scrape the vinegar reduction into a small bowl. Stir in the ketchup, oil, and Tabasco. Transfer to a clean jar with a tight-fitting lid. Store in the refrigerator for up to 3 weeks.

MAKES ABOUT ⅔ CUP

sweet potato tempura

*Try serving guests tempura hot
from the pan. Add some take-out
sushi, and you have a meal.*

1½ cups ice water

1 large egg yolk

1 cup all-purpose flour

½ cup soy sauce

½ cup vegetable broth

1 tablespoon grated
fresh ginger

2 sweet potatoes
(8 to 10 ounces each),
peeled & cut into
⅛-inch-thick slices

Vegetable oil for
deep-frying

IN A MEDIUM-SIZE BOWL, whisk together the water and egg yolk. Whisk in the flour until smooth. Set the bowl over ice.

In a small bowl, combine the soy sauce, broth, and ginger. Set aside.

Soak the potatoes in lukewarm water for 5 minutes. Drain, rinse under cold water, and pat dry. In a large heavy pot with high sides, heat 3 to 4 inches of vegetable oil to 375°F *(see Note, p. 42)*. Pierce a potato slice with a bamboo skewer. Dip into the batter, let the excess drip off, then lower into the hot oil. Remove from the skewer. Repeat with 5 to 7 potato slices (do not crowd them) and fry for 2 to 3 minutes, or until the potatoes are cooked through and the batter is crispy. Drain on paper towels and fry the remaining potato slices. Serve immediately, accompanied by the soy sauce mixture. **SERVES 4**

curried potato croquettes

Croquettes are a French classic, served as a side dish or an appetizer. These croquettes are intensely flavored with hot curry, cumin, and ginger.

1½ pounds baking potatoes, peeled & cut into 1½-inch chunks

4 cups chopped fresh spinach

¾ cup frozen green peas, thawed

½ cup shelled pistachio nuts, chopped

2 large eggs, separated

2 garlic cloves, chopped

2½ teaspoons hot curry powder

1 teaspoon ground cumin

½ teaspoon ground ginger

¼ teaspoon cumin seeds

Salt & freshly ground pepper

2 cups dried bread crumbs

Vegetable oil

I N   A   M E D I U M - S I Z E saucepan, cover the potatoes with water and bring to a boil. Cook over medium heat for 20 minutes, or until tender when pierced with a fork. Drain the potatoes, put them into a large bowl, and mash until smooth.

In a medium-size saucepan, cook the spinach in ½ inch boiling water for 1 to 2 minutes, just until wilted. Drain thoroughly, let cool slightly, then squeeze out as much water as possible.

Add the spinach, peas, pistachios, egg yolks, garlic, curry powder, ground cumin, ginger, and cumin seeds to the potatoes. Use a wooden spoon or rubber spatula to mix until thoroughly combined. Season with salt and pepper.

Shape the croquettes: Roll about 2 tablespoons of the potato mixture into a cylinder, about 3 inches long and 1 inch wide. Set aside.

Place the egg whites and bread crumbs in separate shallow bowls. Beat the egg whites until frothy.

In a large skillet, heat ½ to ¾ inch of oil over medium heat until very hot but not smoking. Meanwhile, dip the croquettes into the egg whites, turning them to make sure they are evenly coated, then roll in the bread crumbs, coating them well. Fry the croquettes, in batches of 6 to 8, turning them once, for about 2 minutes, or until they are an even golden brown. Drain on paper towels. **SERVES 4 TO 6**

T I P

This recipe can be prepared ahead up to the point of frying. The croquettes are also delicious warmed the next day as a snack with spicy ketchup or Asian hot sauce.

perfect hash browns

2 pounds russet or Yukon Gold potatoes, peeled & cut into 1½-inch chunks

5 tablespoons vegetable oil

½ cup chopped onion

Salt & freshly ground pepper

To me, hash browns are fried breakfast potatoes made from cut-up potatoes with lots of chopped onion. The trick to making them really crispy on the outside is to let the oil get sizzling hot before adding the potatoes.

IN A LARGE SAUCEPAN, cover the potatoes with water and bring to a boil. Cook over medium heat for 15 minutes, or until tender when pierced with a fork. Drain the potatoes and let cool for 10 to 15 minutes.

Cut the potatoes into ½-inch pieces. Set aside.

In a large heavy skillet, heat 3 tablespoons of the oil over high heat. Add the onion and saute for about 2 to 3 minutes, or until softened. Add the potatoes to the skillet, spreading them to form an even layer. Season with salt and pepper. Reduce the heat to medium and cook for 4 to 6 minutes, or until the potatoes are browned and crusty on the bottom.

Use a narrow metal spatula to loosen the potatoes from the sides and bottom of the skillet. Invert a large plate over the potatoes and turn the skillet over to remove the potatoes.

Return the skillet to the heat and add the remaining 2 tablespoons oil. When the oil is hot, slide the hash browns back into the skillet, and season with salt and pepper. Cook for 3 to 4 minutes longer, or until the second side is well browned. Slide the hash browns onto a serving platter, or serve them directly from the pan. **SERVES 4 TO 6**

T I P

There are endless variations to these perfect hash browns. As you saute the onions, try adding diced bell pepper or jalapeño chile, diced ham, crumbled bacon, whole corn kernels— or anything else that strikes your fancy!

classic potato pancakes

¾ pound russet potatoes, peeled

¼ cup finely chopped onion

1 large egg

2 tablespoons all-purpose flour

Salt & freshly ground pepper

Peanut or vegetable oil, for pan-frying

When my grandmother made potato pancakes, she made a day of it. Served up from late morning till late afternoon, the ever-hot platter of pancakes was surrounded by pork sausages, lots of homemade applesauce, tangy pickled beets, and thick sour cream.

COARSELY GRATE THE potatoes and put into a medium-size bowl. Stir in the onion, egg, and flour, and season with salt and pepper.

In a large heavy skillet, heat ¼ inch of oil over medium heat until very hot but not smoking. Check the seasoning of the potato mixture by frying about 1 teaspoon of the batter until golden brown on both sides. Taste, and season the potato mixture with additional salt and pepper if needed.

Drop the potato mixture into the skillet by ⅓ cupfuls, flattening them slightly with a spatula. Cook for 2 to 3 minutes, or until crisp and brown on the bottom. Using the spatula, turn the pancakes over and brown the second side. Drain the pancakes briefly on paper towels before serving. (Potato pancakes are best served hot, but they will hold on a paper towel–lined baking sheet in a warm oven for 10 to 15 minutes.)

SERVES 4 TO 6

scallion potato pancakes

Omit the onion and add ¼ cup shredded carrots and 1 tablespoon chopped scallion (green part only) to the potato mixture.

sweet potato pancakes

Use sweet potatoes in place of the baking potatoes and add ¼ cup shredded parsnips to the potato mixture.

T I P

My grandmother always insisted on grating the potatoes by hand for her pancakes, and after some trial and error, I realized she was right. Using a food processor changes the texture of the potatoes; the pancakes don't cook properly and tend to be soggy.

new potatoes with parsley butter

1¾ **pounds tiny new potatoes**

¼ **cup (½ stick) butter**

½ **cup finely chopped fresh parsley**

Salt & freshly ground pepper

When parsley steams in melted butter together with tiny new potatoes, its texture softens and its fresh flavor intensifies. From this trio of simple ingredients comes a heavenly side dish.

IN A LARGE SAUCEPAN, cover the potatoes with water. Bring to a boil and cook over medium heat for 10 to 12 minutes, or until just tender. Drain. When cool enough to handle, peel the potatoes.

In a medium-size saucepan with a tight-fitting lid, melt the butter over medium heat. Add the potatoes and parsley, stirring gently to coat the potatoes. Season with salt and pepper. Reduce the heat to very low, cover, and let the potatoes steam for 1 to 2 minutes before serving. **SERVES 4 TO 6**

mashed sweet potatoes with leeks

Leeks are a member of the onion family, and are known for their delicate flavor. Choose small to medium-size leeks with bright-green leaves and unblemished white portions and be sure to wash them thoroughly.

3 sweet potatoes (about 2 pounds), peeled & cut into 1½-inch chunks

3 tablespoons butter

2 cups julienned leeks (white part only)

3 tablespoons dry white wine

12 Kalamata or other brine-cured olives, halved & pitted

Salt & freshly ground pepper

IN A LARGE SAUCEPAN, cover the potatoes with water and bring to a boil. Reduce the heat to medium and cook for 20 to 25 minutes, or until tender. Drain; return the potatoes to the saucepan and mash until smooth. Set aside.

In a small skillet, melt the butter over medium heat. Add the leeks, saute for 2 to 3 minutes until softened; add the wine.

Stir the leeks, pan juices, and olives into the potatoes. Season with salt and pepper. Reheat over low heat then serve.

SERVES 4 TO 6

perfect mashed potatoes

These are my mother's mashed potatoes. The secret lies in the details: the right variety of potato combined with just the perfect amount of milk and butter.

2 pounds russet or Yukon Gold potatoes, peeled & cut into 1½-inch chunks

¼ cup (½ stick) butter

⅓ cup milk

Salt & freshly ground pepper

IN A LARGE SAUCEPAN, cover the potatoes with water and bring to a boil. Cook over medium heat for about 20 minutes, or until tender when pierced with a fork. Drain the potatoes and set aside.

In the same saucepan, melt the butter over medium heat. Add the milk and heat until little bubbles form around the edges. Return the potatoes to the saucepan, reduce the heat to low, and mash the potatoes with a potato masher until smooth. Season with salt and pepper. Serve immediately.

SERVES 4 TO 6

best home-style gravy

*The best gravy contains pan
    drippings: the juices and fat that
accumulate after roasting a
    turkey, chicken, or beef. Even if
you're not planning to make
    gravy when you roast meat, save
the juices to make some later.*

2 tablespoons fat,
   from pan drippings

2 tablespoons
   all-purpose flour

2¼ cups unsalted chicken
   or beef broth

2 to 4 tablespoons
   pan juices

Salt & freshly ground
   pepper

IN A MEDIUM-SIZE SAUCEPAN, melt the fat over medium heat. Whisk in the flour, stirring vigorously to form a paste. Gradually pour in the broth, whisking constantly, until the gravy thickens, boils, and no lumps remain. Add the pan juices. Reduce the heat to low and simmer, stirring often, for 3 to 4 minutes. Season with salt and pepper. Serve immediately. **MAKES ABOUT 2½ CUPS**

low-fat mashed potatoes

This may be a low-fat dish, but it's certainly high in flavor. The chicken broth takes the place of butter or cream, and the herbs add an unexpected freshness.

2 pounds russet or Yukon Gold potatoes, peeled & cut into 1½-inch chunks

1 cup chicken broth (any visible fat removed) or vegetable broth

2 tablespoons chopped fresh parsley

2 teaspoons chopped fresh thyme

Salt & freshly ground pepper

IN A LARGE SAUCEPAN, cover the potatoes with water and bring to a boil. Cook over medium heat for about 20 minutes, or until easily pierced with a fork. Drain the potatoes, return them to the saucepan, and mash until smooth. Gradually add the broth, stirring until the potatoes are smooth. Stir in the parsley and thyme and season with salt and pepper. Serve immediately. **SERVES 4 TO 6**

basil mashed potatoes

Most mashed potato recipes call for butter and cream, but here olive oil and lots of fragrant basil provide the texture and flavor. Use a really good-quality olive oil; its flavor will shine through.

2 pounds russet or Yukon Gold potatoes, peeled & cut into large chunks

½ cup coarsely chopped fresh basil

⅓ cup olive oil, preferably extra-virgin

3 tablespoons dry white wine or chicken broth

Salt & freshly ground pepper

IN A LARGE SAUCEPAN, cover the potatoes with water and bring to a boil. Cook over medium heat for 20 minutes, or until tender when pierced with a fork. Drain the potatoes and return them to the saucepan. Stir in the basil, oil, and wine. Mash the potatoes, using a potato masher, until no lumps remain. Season with salt and pepper, mixing well. **SERVES 4 TO 6**

garlic smashed potatoes

2 **pounds russet potatoes,
peeled & coarsely chopped**

½ **cup milk**

5 **tablespoons butter,
cut into pieces**

6 **to 8 roasted garlic cloves,
peeled** *(see Note)*

Salt & freshly ground pepper

2 **tablespoons vegetable oil**

⅔ **cup thinly sliced shallots**

NOTE

*To roast garlic, place a whole,
unpeeled head of garlic in a
custard cup; drizzle with
1 tablespoon olive oil. Cover
tightly with foil. Bake in a
375°F oven for 30 minutes,
or until softened.*

*This side dish is a study in
contrasts. The coarsely mashed potatoes
are accented by creamy sweet
roasted garlic, and the fried shallots
piled on top add crunch
and a delicate onion flavor.*

IN A MEDIUM-SIZE SAUCEPAN,
cover the potatoes with water and bring to a boil. Cook
over medium heat for 20 minutes, or until tender when
pierced with a fork.

Drain the potatoes and return them to the saucepan. Add
the milk, butter, and garlic. Use a potato masher to mash the
potatoes very roughly. They should look "smashed" and just
hold together. Season with salt and pepper. Keep warm.

In a small skillet, heat the oil until very hot. Add the
shallots, in small batches, and fry for 15 to 20 seconds, or until
browned and crisp. To serve, mound the smashed potatoes in
a heated serving bowl and top with the frizzled shallots.

SERVES 4 TO 6

truly decadent
mashed potatoes

2 pounds russet or Yukon Gold potatoes, peeled & cut into 1½-inch chunks (about 5 cups)

¾ cup (1½ sticks) unsalted butter

¾ cup heavy cream

Salt & freshly ground pepper

Butter and cream supply the decadence. Using a potato ricer guarantees an absolutely smooth texture.

IN A LARGE SAUCEPAN, cover the potatoes with water and bring to a boil. Cook over medium heat for about 20 minutes, or until easily pierced with a fork. Drain. Use a potato ricer to puree the potatoes into a large bowl. Set aside.

In the same saucepan, melt the butter over medium heat. Add the cream. When the mixture begins to simmer, add the potatoes. Reduce the heat to low and stir until smooth and heated through. Season with salt and pepper. Serve immediately. **SERVES 4 TO 6**

white truffle oil mashed potatoes

Just before serving, add 3 to 4 tablespoons white truffle oil (available in specialty food stores) to the potatoes. Pass additional truffle oil to drizzle over the potatoes.

potato & celery root puree

This dish is elegant and sophisticated, a subtle balance of potato and delicate celery flavors, deliciously enriched with browned butter.

IN SEPARATE MEDIUM-SIZE saucepans, cover the potatoes and celery root with water and bring to a boil. Cook over medium heat for about 20 minutes, or until tender when pierced with a fork. Drain.

Meanwhile, in a small saucepan, cook the butter over medium heat until foamy. Continue to cook for 1 to 2 minutes longer, or until the butter turns a nutty brown. Transfer immediately to a small bowl.

Use a potato ricer or food mill to puree the potatoes and celery root. Put the puree into a medium-size saucepan and set over low heat. Stir in the half-and-half, celery seeds, and nutmeg. Add the browned butter, discarding the milk solids in the bottom of the bowl, and stir until well blended. Season with salt and pepper. Serve immediately. **SERVES 4 TO 6**

1½ pounds russet or Yukon Gold potatoes, peeled & cut into 1-inch chunks

1 cup peeled & coarsely chopped celery root

5 tablespoons butter

½ cup half-and-half, heated

⅛ teaspoon celery seeds

Pinch of grated nutmeg

Salt & freshly ground pepper

thanksgiving sweet potatoes

3 sweet potatoes (about
   2 pounds), peeled & cut
   into 1½-inch chunks

3 tablespoons butter, cut
   into small pieces

¼ cup dry sherry

⅓ cup coarsely chopped
   dried cranberries

1 tablespoon freshly
   grated orange zest

1 tablespoon coarsely
   chopped candied ginger

Salt & freshly ground
   pepper

Orange zest strips,
   for garnish

The brilliant orange of the sweet potato puree, flecked with deep-red dried cranberries make this a colorful holiday side dish. It pairs well with roasted turkey, chile-rubbed pork tenderloin, or corn bread stuffed Cornish hens.

IN A LARGE SAUCEPAN, cover the potatoes with water and bring to a boil. Cook over medium heat for 20 to 25 minutes, or until tender.

In a food processor, combine the potatoes, butter, and sherry, and process until smooth. Transfer to a heated serving bowl and stir in the cranberries, grated orange zest, and ginger. Season with salt and pepper, garnish with orange zest strips, and serve. **SERVES 4 TO 6**

sweet potatoes with chipotles

*These candied sweet potatoes get
their kick from the contrast between
hot, smoky chipotle chiles and
sweet apple cider and brown sugar.*

3 sweet potatoes (about
  2 pounds), peeled & cut
  into ¼-inch-thick slices

¼ cup (½ stick) butter

¾ cup apple cider

3 tablespoons packed
  brown sugar

2 chipotle chiles en adobo,
  coarsely chopped,
  plus 2 tablespoons
  adobo sauce

Salt & freshly ground
  pepper

⅓ cup salted roasted
  pumpkin seeds,
  coarsely chopped

PREHEAT THE OVEN
to 375°F. In a large saucepan, cover the potatoes with water
and bring to a boil. Cook over medium heat for 12 to 15
minutes, or until tender. Drain.

Meanwhile, in a medium-size skillet, melt the butter over
medium heat. Whisk in the apple cider and brown sugar. Cook
for 2 minutes, whisking, until the sugar has dissolved. Stir in
the chipotles and adobo sauce, season with salt and pepper,
and set aside.

In a shallow round baking dish, arrange the potatoes in
concentric circles, slightly overlapping the slices. Pour the cider-
chipotle sauce over them.

Bake for 30 to 35 minutes, or until the sauce is thick and
the potatoes are browned. Sprinkle with the pumpkin seeds.
Serve immediately. **SERVES 4 TO 6**

winter potatoes anna

Traditionally, pommes Anna are made from baking potatoes, but here spirals of thinly sliced white potatoes are alternated with sweet potatoes and winter squash.

P R E H E A T   T H E   O V E N to 425°F. Place the oven rack in the center of the oven.

Generously brush a 9-inch glass pie plate with 2 tablespoons of the melted butter. Set aside.

Cut the potatoes and sweet potato into ⅛-inch-thick slices. Soak the baking potato and the sweet potato in separate bowls of lukewarm water for 2 to 3 minutes. Drain and rinse well. Dry thoroughly and wrap in a clean kitchen towel.

Beginning in the center of the pie plate, arrange the Yukon Gold potatoes in slightly overlapping concentric circles to form the first layer. Generously brush with some of the melted butter. Season with salt and pepper. Form a second layer in the same manner, alternating sweet potato and butternut

½ cup plus 2 tablespoons (1¼ sticks) unsalted butter, melted

1¼ pounds Yukon Gold potatoes, peeled

1 sweet potato (8 ounces), peeled

Salt & freshly ground pepper

½ small butternut squash (about 8 ounces), peeled, seeded, & cut crosswise into ⅛-inch-thick slices

squash slices. Wedge in any odd-shaped slices of squash, and press the layers down with a metal spatula. Brush with butter and season with salt and pepper. Use the remaining potato slices to form the top layer. Press the layers firmly. Brush with the remaining butter and season with salt and pepper. Place a square of foil over the potatoes. Put a small heavy skillet or pot on top of the foil to weight the potatoes.

Bake the potatoes in the center of the oven for 25 minutes. Remove the weight and the foil. Continue to bake for 20 to 25 minutes, or until it is golden brown and the potatoes and squash are tender. Let rest for 5 minutes. Use a long metal spatula to carefully loosen the potatoes from the sides and bottom of the pie plate. Invert a serving plate over the potatoes. Carefully invert the potato cake onto the plate. Cut into wedges and serve immediately. **SERVES 6**

TIP

Make sure you weight the potatoes properly during baking to create a cake that is crispy on the outside and soft in the center.

romesco roasted potatoes

½ cup olive oil

¾ cup fresh bread crumbs

1 roasted yellow bell pepper, peeled, cored, seeded & cut into ½-inch-wide strips

1 plum tomato, coarsely chopped

¼ cup almonds, toasted

1 garlic clove, chopped

¼ to ½ teaspoon crushed red pepper flakes

3 tablespoons red wine vinegar

Salt & freshly ground pepper

1¾ pounds small new potatoes, scrubbed

Romesco, a Mediterranean sauce, blends roasted peppers, tomatoes, olive oil, garlic, and toasted almonds in a sauce that has the consistency of a thick, chunky mayonnaise.

PREHEAT THE OVEN to 375°F. In a small skillet, heat 2 tablespoons of the oil over medium heat. Add the breadcrumbs, and cook, stirring, until golden. Transfer to a food processor. Add the bell pepper, tomato, almonds, garlic, and red pepper flakes, pulsing. Add the vinegar and ¼ cup of the oil. Pulse until the mixture forms a chunky paste. Season with salt and pepper. Set aside.

Halve the potatoes lengthwise and cut each half into 3 wedges. Put into a shallow baking dish and toss with the remaining 2 tablespoons oil, then arrange in a single layer. Roast the potatoes for 20 minutes. Add the romesco, stirring to coat evenly. Roast for 10 to 15 minutes longer, or until tender and the romesco becomes crusty. Serve hot. **SERVES 4 TO 6**

provençal grilled potatoes

Tapenade, a condiment that originated in the south of France, is a paste made from olives, garlic, anchovies, and capers. It's often served on bread or as a dip for vegetables.

PREHEAT A GAS GRILL to medium or prepare a medium-hot charcoal fire.

In a large saucepan, cover the potatoes with water and bring to a boil. Cook over medium heat for 15 minutes, or until almost cooked through. Drain. Put the potatoes into a large bowl with the onion and toss with the oil.

Prepare the tapenade: In a food processor, combine all the ingredients except the oil, salt, and pepper. Process, slowly adding the oil, until smooth. Set aside.

Grill the potatoes and onions, turning occasionally, for 3 to 4 minutes, or until tender. Transfer to a bowl. Separate the onion layers. Add the tapenade, season with salt and pepper, and gently toss. Serve at room temperature. **SERVES 4 TO 6**

1¾ pounds new potatoes, scrubbed & quartered

1 medium-size red onion, quartered

2 tablespoons olive oil

TAPENADE

3 tablespoons coarsely chopped fresh parsley

2 tablespoons fresh lemon juice

1 tablespoon olive paste

1 garlic clove, halved

2 teaspoons capers

1 teaspoon anchovy paste

3 tablespoons olive oil

Salt & freshly ground pepper

roasted potatoes with lemon

I'm always looking for new ways to cook tiny sunburst squash, and this is one of the best. Lemon zest and lemon juice provide the light flavor of summer.

- 1¾ pounds small new potatoes, scrubbed
- 4 to 6 small yellow sunburst or pattypan squash (about 2 inches in diameter), quartered
- 3 tablespoons olive oil
- 2 tablespoons finely chopped fresh parsley
- 1 tablespoon grated lemon zest
- 1 tablespoon fresh lemon juice
- Salt & freshly ground pepper
- 2 to 3 ounces imported Parmesan or Asiago cheese, shaved with a vegetable peeler into paper-thin slices

PREHEAT THE OVEN to 375°F. Halve the potatoes lengthwise, then cut each half into 3 wedges. Put the potatoes and squash into a shallow baking dish, toss with the oil, and arrange in a single layer.

Roast the vegetables for 30 to 35 minutes, or until browned and tender, turning them over after 15 minutes. Toss with the parsley, lemon zest, and lemon juice. Season with salt and pepper. Transfer to a serving bowl and top with the Parmesan shavings. **SERVES 4 TO 6**

Photograph on page 2

sweet potato pecan muffins

Sweet potatoes are often prepared with lots of sugar, especially in the South—one old recipe calls for baking several pounds of potatoes with five cups of sugar! This recipe takes a more moderate approach.

PREHEAT THE OVEN to 375°F. Line a 12-cup muffin tin with paper liners or grease the muffin cups.

Prepare the pecan streusel topping: In a medium-size bowl, combine all the ingredients except the butter. Use your fingertips to work in the butter until the mixture is crumbly and forms tiny pea-size clumps. Set aside.

Prepare the muffin batter: In a large bowl, whisk the flour, brown sugar, baking soda, baking powder, salt, cinnamon, nutmeg, and allspice. In a medium-size bowl, whisk the sweet potato, eggs, vegetable oil, and milk until blended. Pour the

PECAN STREUSEL TOPPING

- ⅓ cup coarsely chopped pecans
- ¼ cup all-purpose flour
- 3 tablespoons packed brown sugar
- 1 tablespoon sugar
- ¼ teaspoon ground cinnamon
- ¼ teaspoon grated nutmeg
- 1 tablespoon cold butter

liquid ingredients over the dry and stir with a rubber spatula just until combined; do not overmix.

Spoon the batter into the prepared cups, filling them three-quarters full. Sprinkle about 1 tablespoon of the pecan streusel topping over each muffin.

Bake the muffins for 25 minutes, or until the tops spring back when lightly pressed, or a toothpick inserted into the center comes out clean. Place the muffin pan on a wire rack for 5 minutes, then remove the muffins to the wire rack. Serve warm or at room temperature. These muffins keep well for several days. Store in an airtight container at room temperature, or for longer storage, in the freezer for up to 3 weeks. **MAKES 12 MUFFINS**

MUFFINS

1 ¾ cups all-purpose flour

¾ cup packed brown sugar

1 teaspoon baking soda

¼ teaspoon baking powder

½ teaspoon salt

½ teaspoon ground cinnamon

¼ teaspoon grated nutmeg

⅛ teaspoon ground allspice

1 sweet potato (8 ounces), cooked & mashed

2 large eggs

⅓ cup vegetable oil

⅓ cup milk

index